Rocky Mountain
Wildlife

Text and Photography
by David Dahms

The red-tailed hawk is the most common soaring hawk in North America, named for its rust-colored tail. This dark phase bird is a variation of the more typical lighter plumage.

Front cover:
Rocky Mountain bighorn ram

Title page:
Mountain goat kid in tundra flowers

Opposite page:
Mountain bluebird

Back cover:
Mountain goat kids
Mountain lion kitten
Red fox kit

Published by
Paragon Press
991 Ridge West Drive
Windsor, CO 80550

www.paragon-press.com

ISBN 0-9646359-0-9

Printed in Korea

Table of Contents

Bull elk bugling in frosty meadow

Elk calf

ELK (also called **WAPITI**)

Elk are the second largest members of the deer family. They live in open forests and mountain meadow areas. They are brown or tan with a darker belly, about five feet tall at the shoulder. Male elk (bulls) weigh up to 1000 pounds and female (cow) elk weigh about 550 pounds. Bulls lose their antlers in the spring and grow a new, larger set each summer, nourished by a blood-rich, fuzzy covering called velvet. As the autumn mating season approaches, the velvet dries and falls off. The largest bulls gather harems of many cows and defend them from other challengers. Usually the intruder is repelled by a threat or a charge, but sometimes the two bulls lock antlers and hold a spectacular pushing and shoving match. Bulls also announce their presence by bugling, a bellowing, whistling sound. Elk mainly eat grass, and when food is scarce in the winter, they eat aspen bark, leaving dark scars on the trunks. Elk are best viewed at dawn and dusk, since they spend their days bedded down among the trees.

Bull elk with antlers in velvet

5

Mule deer buck

Mule deer bucks fighting

MULE DEER

Mule deer are the most common and widespread large mammal in the Rockies, named for their large mule-like ears. Mule deer are stockier than their eastern relative, the white-tailed deer, standing about three feet tall and averaging 200 pounds, with a brown or gray coat. They live mostly in mountain areas, but sometimes in cities and towns. Male deer (bucks) shed their antlers and grow a new set each year. During the mating season in November, a buck will search for a receptive female (doe) and defend her from other suitors. A threatening display usually repels the smaller buck, otherwise they join antlers and engage in a violent twisting and shoving battle. Fawns are born in June. Their spotted coats and lack of scent helps conceal them from predators. They spend their first few days hidden while their mother feeds nearby, returning periodically to nurse. Mule deer are best spotted at dawn and dusk, since they spend their days resting in the forest.

Mule deer fawn

Cow moose with twin calves

MOOSE

Moose are the largest members of the deer family. These huge animals stand about seven feet at the shoulder and weigh up to 1200 pounds. Their overhanging upper lip, long muzzles and peculiar gait gives them an ungainly appearance. Males (bulls) grow massive broadly flattened palmate antlers, four to five feet wide. Moose are dark brown, with long pale legs. Those long legs allow them to wade in lakes and streams where they feed on aquatic vegetation and nearby willows. In the autumn mating season, a bull will spend a week with one cow, then move on. During this period, hormone-crazed bulls can be unpredictable and dangerous. Moose inhabit the northern Rockies, and have been reintroduced into their former ranges in northern and southern Colorado.

Bull moose

Bighorn ewe and ram

BIGHORN SHEEP

Bighorn sheep are magnificent animals, famous for their dramatic head-butting battles. They are tan or dark brown with a white rump patch, and are excellent rock climbers. Both sexes have horns. The female (ewe) has short, slightly curved horns, while the male (ram) has the familiar heavy curling horns. Horns are never shed, but continue to grow throughout the ram's life, reaching a full curl after about eight years. Horns are made of keratin, the same hard protein that forms hooves and hair. Bighorns have reinforced skulls and strong necks to withstand the impact of their fights. In the summer, they stay in high mountain areas, rams separate from the ewes. When the snow falls and November mating season approaches, bighorns move down to their traditional ranges and the rams join the ewes. The dominant ram searches continuously for a receptive ewe and tries to discourage other eager rams. Bighorn social status centers on horn size and rams have a complex system of body language to maintain hierarchy. When that fails they resort to their well-known horn-clashing battles.

Bighorn ram

Mountain goat nanny and kid

MOUNTAIN GOAT

Mountain goats are wooly white animals that live in the highest mountain areas. With their spongy hooves and muscular shoulders, they are champion mountaineers. They are smaller than they appear, only about three feet tall. Both the male (billy) and female (nanny) have thin sharp black horns, and it is difficult to tell them apart. Kids are born in late spring on precipitous cliffs, safe from predators. They can walk in a few days, and spend their first summer frolicking among rocks in their alpine playground. When the winter snows blow, a billy will search for a nanny, approaching her cautiously. Unlike most animals, a nanny will attack an annoying billy until she is ready to mate. Mountain goats stay on their lofty ranges all winter, relying on their shaggy white coats to protect them from winter's icy cold. They forage for food on wind-blown, south-facing slopes, steadfastly awaiting the warmer days of spring.

Mountain goats naturally range in northern Montana and Idaho, and have been transplanted into certain areas of other western states. The easiest place to see them is on Mount Evans west of Denver and in Glacier National Park in Montana.

Mountain goat kids

13

Pronghorn buck

PRONGHORN

Pronghorn are the fastest North American land animal, capable of speeds up to 70 MPH. They are sometimes called "antelope" or "pronghorn antelope" although they are not related to true antelopes at all. They live on wide open plains, where their excellent eyesight and speed are their primary defenses. At full speed they run with a twenty foot stride, yet cannot jump over a three foot fence and are forced to crawl under it. Pronghorn are about three feet tall, with coats of brown and white hair, and a white rump patch. When alarmed, the rump hairs stand on end, making it look twice as large. Both males (bucks) and females (does) have curved black horns. There is a distinct prong at the center of the horn, hence the name pronghorn. The outer sheath of the horns is shed each year, but a bony core remains. Fawns are born in the spring, lying secluded in tall grass for the first few days while mother grazes at a distance.

Pronghorn doe and fawn

Black bear in autumn snow shower

BLACK BEAR
GRIZZLY BEAR

Bears are the largest terrestrial carnivores, although the majority of their diet is vegetarian. They are opportunistic feeders, eating twigs, nuts, roots, berries, grubs, ants, squirrels, honey, fish and carrion. Careless human garbage attracts bears, who soon become a dangerous nuisance. They go to underground dens and appear to hibernate in winter, but their body temperatures do not drop like true hibernators. Grizzly bears weigh 400-1000 pounds, with a concave profile and humped shoulders. Their range has been reduced to the northern Rocky Mountains and Yellowstone National Park, plus parts of Canada and Alaska. Black bears are smaller, 200 to 600 pounds, with a flat face. They live throughout the Rockies. Both grizzlies and black bears may be black, brown or cinnamon. Black bears can climb trees, to feed or escape from other bears. Tiny cubs weighing less than a pound are born in the winter while the mother is asleep in her den. They will stay with their mother for two years.

Grizzly bear

Mountain lion kitten

MOUNTAIN LION

Mountain lions are secretive large cats, also called cougar, puma, panther, or catamount. They are tawny brown, and weigh 75-200 pounds. Mountain lions are strong, stealthy, nocturnal hunters that feed primarily on deer. A stalking lion will approach unnoticed, creeping forward slowly and silently within 30 feet of its prey before pouncing on its back and biting its neck. The lion will eat as much as it can, then cover the remains with leaves and branches until it returns to eat more. Each male lion has a large territory which it defends from other males. Since they are so sparsely distributed and mostly nocturnal, they are rarely seen by humans, though sightings are becoming more common as deer move into suburbs and people move into the foothills. Kittens are born in midsummer, and nurse for the first month before their introduction to meat. The young stay with their mother as long as two years while she teaches them to hunt, before heading out on their own.

Mountain lion

19

Red Fox

RED FOX

Red foxes are relatives of coyotes and wolves in the dog family. They are surprisingly small, less than 15 pounds. They are usually the familiar orange-red color, but sometimes are partially or completely black or silver, all with a huge fluffy tail with a white tip. Foxes use the same trails each night as they search for food. Their diet is primarily mice, but includes grass, nuts, fruit and insects as well as small animals like voles, rabbits and squirrels. Foxes were imported from England for the sport of riding with the hounds. They live in agricultural as well as forested areas, and sometimes in open urban areas. A fox generally won't use a den to escape winter's cold. Instead it will curl up in a ball, wrapped in its own bushy tail.

Young red fox

Coyote

COYOTE

Coyotes are common predators throughout the west. They are generally gray, 20 to 40 pounds, and members of the dog family. Coyotes are known for their haunting nighttime howling. They are extremely adaptable, living anywhere from marshy river bottoms to high alpine tundra. Coyotes have a widely variable and opportunistic diet, dining on small animals, frogs, birds, fruit, plants and carrion. They often hunt rodents by pouncing on them, and several coyotes may team up to attack larger prey like deer. Coyote pups are born in the spring in an underground den. They are weaned after six weeks, but stay with their parents for six to nine months. Like most predators, coyotes are despised by ranchers for preying on livestock. But in spite of efforts to control them, the coyote population is still increasing.

Coyote

Gray wolf

GRAY WOLF

The gray wolf is a large, powerful predator that resembles a giant dog. It may be gray, black, or white, and weigh 60 - 130 pounds. Its huge paws leave impressive tracks, four to five inches long. Wolves are social animals, living in groups of up to 15 members. Many types of howls are used to communicate among the members of the pack. Wolves feed mostly on large mammals, preferring a sickly weak animal over a healthy one. Sometimes they work together to ambush their prey. In each pack only the dominant male and female breed, and then the whole group takes care of the pups. Gray wolves have been reintroduced to Yellowstone National Park and central Idaho through a controversial reintroduction plan.

Gray wolf

Pika

PIKA

The tiny pika lives on talus rock-piles in high mountain areas. They are mostly brown, with tiny ears and no tail. In the summer months, pikas are easily seen scurrying among the rocks. They busily collect mouthfuls of plants and spread them under the talus to dry. When not foraging, they perch on prominent rocks and watch for predators. If threatened, they emit a loud squeak, alerting other pikas in the area. Pikas are related to rabbits and hares, so they do not hibernate in winter. Instead they live among the talus, under the mantle of snow, eating their cache of dried plants.

Pika with mouthful of greens

Yellow-bellied marmot family

YELLOW-BELLIED MARMOT

Yellow-bellied marmots are large, dark brown rodents that live on talus slopes high in the mountains. A similar species is the larger hoary marmot, which is silver-gray and lives north of central Montana. They are nicknamed "whistle pigs" for their distinctive whistles. They spend the short alpine summer gorging on green vegetation and sunning themselves on convenient rock outcroppings. Young marmots are born in the spring, and will be fully grown by fall. By the end of summer, they will have added 60% to their body weight, giving them a comical, pudgy appearance. Marmots pass the long winter hibernating in underground burrows, awaiting the warmer days of summer.

Young yellow-bellied marmot

Raccoon

RACCOON

The raccoon is a widespread and well known creature, distinguished by its bushy ringed tail and its familiar facial mask. Raccoons have a widely varied diet, feeding on things such as fruit, nuts, insects, mice, eggs, frogs, and fish. They readily exploit suburban areas, raiding garbage cans and gardens at night. Raccoons appear to wash their food since much of it is found near water, however other things are eaten dry. Raccoons mate in the winter, and the female makes a nest in a tree cavity and gives birth to 4 to 5 young in May. They are on their own by autumn, off to rattle other garbage cans in the night.

LONG-TAILED WEASEL

Weasels are energetic, fearless small carnivores that live in rocky and brushy areas. Their sinuous bodies seem to flow over the ground as they relentlessly search for food. They prey mainly on mice, plus pikas, rabbits, birds and squirrels, climbing trees and boldly attacking animals several times their size. They must eat a lot to support their high-speed lifestyle. Male weasels are almost twice as large as females, up to 21" long. The short-tailed weasel is very similar, but about half as large. Both species are brown with a light belly. In the winter, they turn completely white with a black tip on their tails.

Long-tailed Weasel

River Otter

RIVER OTTER

The river otter is a fun-loving member of the weasel family. It is a powerful swimmer with a streamlined body and strong tail. Its dark brown coat of thick, oily fur insulates it from icy waters in winter. Because of this beautiful durable fur, it was nearly trapped out of existence in the 1800's. Otters feed primarily on fish, plus crayfish and small mammals. Anglers may not appreciate the competition for fish, though otters prefer slower-moving rough fish. Otters are playful animals, amusing themselves by body surfing in rushing water and sliding on snow. They get a running start before sliding down their snow chute, only to scamper back uphill and do it all again.

River Otter

Mountain Cottontail

MOUNTAIN COTTONTAIL

The Mountain Cottontail (also Nuttall's Cottontail) is the most common rabbit in the Rocky Mountains. It is gray-brown with short black-tipped ears. It uses a burrow or rocky crevice for shelter, plus a shallow sheltered depression in the ground called a "form." Cottontails are a food source for many other predators. They balance their high mortality rate with prodigious reproduction. One female cottontail can have five litters of 3 to 8 young each year, born blind and naked in a hair-lined nest.

SNOWSHOE HARE

The Snowshoe Hare gets its name from its extra-large hind feet. Snowshoe hares are larger than cottontails, but one of the smallest hares. In the summer its coat is brown. As winter approaches, the shorter daylight hours cause it to gradually shed its old brown coat and replace it with a white one. The cycle is reversed in the spring. If the weather cooperates, the hare is nicely camouflaged in winter's snow and summer's forest. Snowshoe hares produce 2 or 3 litters of about three young each year. They are born fully-furred, eyes open, and able to move about within hours. The population of snowshoe hares is cyclical, climbing for 9 or 10 years before suddenly plummeting.

Snowshoe hare beginning its spring molt

Golden-mantled Ground Squirrel

Least Chipmunk

GOLDEN-MANTLED GROUND SQUIRREL

The golden-mantled ground squirrel is named for the golden color of its head and neck. It has two white stripes with black edges on its back, but none on its face. It fills its cheek pouches with fruit and nuts, and stores the food in its underground burrow. These squirrels become tame around humans and boldly beg for food.

LEAST CHIPMUNK

Chipmunks are fleet-footed and appealing small animals. They can be distinguished from ground squirrels because they have stripes on their heads. Chipmunks are active in the daytime, scampering over rocks and trees, feeding on seeds and berries. The Least Chipmunk is common throughout the Rockies. There are several other species of chipmunks that look very similar. All chipmunks hibernate through the winter in their underground burrows.

WYOMING GROUND SQUIRREL

The Wyoming Ground Squirrel is a medium sized squirrel with a drab coat and no stripes at all. They are nicknamed "picket pins" due to their habit of standing up on their hind legs to survey their surroundings. They eat insects and vegetation, accumulating fat for their winter hibernation. They were formerly called Richardson's Ground Squirrels.

Wyoming Ground Squirrel

37

ABERT'S SQUIRREL

Abert's squirrels are gray or black tree squirrels with distinctive tufted ears. They are highly dependent on ponderosa pine forests. They feed on many parts of the ponderosa pine, including bark and cones. Mating occurs in the spring, males tormenting each other and pursuing females through the treetops. Nests are built high in the trees of grass, sticks, pine needles and bark. They do not hibernate and remain active through the winter. They carry pine cones to favorite spots to eat them, leaving a pile of husks on the ground below.

Abert's Squirrel

PORCUPINE

The porcupine is North America's second largest rodent, famous for its defensive quills. Never in a hurry, it is protected from predators by about 30,000 sharp quills up to five inches long, plus an insulating coat of yellowish long hair. Quills are modified hairs, with tiny barbs at the tip. A porcupine cannot shoot its quills. Instead it swings its tail at its attacker, and when it hits, the loosely anchored quills are driven into the enemy. The barbs pull the quills further into the victim and make removal painful, while they absorb body fluids and swell. Only the fisher can consistently outsmart this prickly defense, flipping the porcupine on its back and attacking its vulnerable belly. In the summer, porcupines eat green plants, and in the winter they feed on inner bark of trees. They are also fond of salt, and munch on tool handles which have absorbed human perspiration. Baby porcupines are born in late spring. Their soft quills are fully formed, and quickly harden. Only one baby is born each year, indicating the effectiveness of porcupines' defenses.

Porcupine

Bald Eagle

Pair of bald eagles

BALD EAGLE

Bald eagles are large, majestic birds with unmistakable white heads and tails. They are about 30 inches tall, weigh around 12 pounds, with a seven foot wingspan. As with all raptors, females are larger than males. Bald eagles primarily eat fish, snatching them from the water with their large talons, plus waterfowl, rodents and carrion. Most bald eagles migrate north into Canada for the summer, but a few remain in the continental United States to nest. Bald eagles mate for life, returning to the same area each year to raise their brood of two chicks. Young eagles do not develop their distinctive white heads until they are 3 to 5 years old.

GOLDEN EAGLE

The golden eagle is a bird of mountains and high plains. It has dark brown plumage with golden feathers on the nape of its neck. It is roughly the same size as the bald eagle, and more common. Golden eagles hunt small and young mammals and rodents, plus grouse, snakes and carrion. A pair of golden eagles will mate for life, and build their nest in a tree or on a cliff. Each year they return and use the same nest, raising four chicks.

Golden Eagle

Great Horned Owl

Great Horned Owl chick

GREAT HORNED OWL
SHORT-EARED OWL

Owls are fascinating and mysterious birds of prey. They are admirably equipped for nocturnal hunting of rodents and small mammals. They have extraordinary hearing and extremely sensitive large eyes to locate their prey in the dark. Their eyes are fixed in their sockets, so they shift their gaze by moving their whole head. Owls have very flexible necks, which allow them to turn their heads 180° left or right, plus upside down. Their ear tufts are just feathers—the ear openings are near their eyes on the edge of the facial disk. The wing feathers of owls have serrated edges so they fly silently. The business end of an owl is its formidable talons, long, sharp and powerful. After a successful hunt, owls gulp down their food. Their weak digestive systems cannot handle bones and hair, so these collect into pellets which are regurgitated.

Great horned owls are familiar and common large owls, about 24" tall with a four foot wingspan. They do not migrate, and begin nesting in mid-winter. They choose from existing nests rather than build new ones. The female incubates the eggs while the male feeds her. The chicks hatch in about a month, covered with fuzzy down. The mother owl may stay in the nest, shielding her chicks from inclement weather with her wings. They grow quickly, fed by both parents, and soon venture out of the nest to a nearby branch. Smaller and less common, short-eared owls nest in April in secluded depressions on the ground.

Short-eared Owl

43

Burrowing Owl

Burrowing owl spinning its head, part of its preening

BURROWING OWL

Burrowing owls are comical little birds with stubby tails and long legs. Unlike other owls, they are active mostly in the daytime. They live on open plains and grasslands of the west, where they are seen perched on fenceposts or standing on the ground. When agitated, they bob up and down, earning the nickname "howdy-do owl." They feed on insects, mice, lizards and snakes. Burrowing owls nest underground, often adapting abandoned prairie dog holes. They tolerate nearby prairie dogs, but do not share underground tunnels with them. Seven to nine eggs are incubated by both parents, and the fluffy chicks hatch in early summer. They soon peek from their hole, but dive back in at the slightest threat. Burrowing owls can imitate the sound of a rattlesnake to discourage predators.

AMERICAN KESTREL

The American Kestrel (also called Sparrow Hawk) is the smallest member of the falcon family. These colorful common birds are often seen perched on telephone poles and wires. Kestrels have rust-colored tails and backs, and two stripes on their heads. Males have slate-blue wings while females have rusty wings. They hunt from high vantage points, or while hovering in mid-air, and dive to the ground to dine on insects or mice. Kestrels nest in tree cavities. The male feeds the female while she incubates the eggs, and mainly feeds the chicks after they hatch. Kestrels can be seen year-round, patiently watching for their next meal.

American Kestrel

45

BROAD-TAILED HUMMINGBIRD

Hummingbirds are the smallest North American birds. They are acrobatic and precise aviators, capable of flying forward and backward, up and down, or hovering in place. They use their long, thin bills and tongues to reach deep into flowers and sip nectar. Their wings normally beat 50 times per second, or up to 200 times per second during courtship flight. The broad-tailed species is about four inches long and is the common nesting hummingbird of the Rockies. They are metallic green, and males have red throats. In the spring, males perform their enticing flight display to attract females. The female builds her tiny nest from bits of lichen, bark, grass and spider webs, then lays and incubates two tiny eggs. It is about two inches across, usually built on a conifer branch. After the chicks hatch, she collects nectar and insects to feed them, with no help from the male. At the first hint of autumn, hummingbirds head south for the winter in Mexico.

Broad-tailed hummingbird at nest

STELLER'S JAY

The Steller's Jay is closely related to the eastern Blue Jay, and similarly noisy and boisterous. They are readily identified by their blue bodies and black heads with distinctive crests. They are common in coniferous forests, where they feed on seeds, berries and insects. They are often seen around picnic areas, begging for a handout. Steller's jays build their treetop nests in May, and the chicks hatch by June. These conspicuous jays can be seen all year, adding a spot of color to a drab winter day.

Steller's Jay

Male Mountain Bluebird   Female Mountain Bluebird

MOUNTAIN BLUEBIRD
WESTERN BLUEBIRD

Brightly colored bluebirds are fairly common and popular songbirds of the forests and meadows of the Rocky Mountains. Western bluebirds prefer the lower elevations while mountain bluebirds like the higher areas. The male mountain bluebird is sky blue with a pale blue belly. The male western bluebird has deep blue wings and head, with an orange breast and a pale belly. The females are mostly gray with subdued blue wings and tail. The males arrive early in the spring to claim suitable nest cavities in trees or boxes. A male's bright blue coloring and potential nest site hopefully attracts a female. She will lay 4 to 6 pale blue eggs and incubate them while he waits patiently nearby, occasionally bringing food to her. After the eggs hatch, both parents busily forage for insects to feed their hungry brood.

Male Western Bluebird

White-breasted Nuthatch

Mountain Chickadee

WHITE-BREASTED NUTHATCH

Nuthatches are acrobatic tree-climbing birds. They are usually seen crawling head first down tree trunks, searching for hidden insects. The white-breasted nuthatch is about six inches long and nests in a tree cavity. Similar species are the Red-breasted Nuthatch with its rust-colored belly, and the smaller Pygmy Nuthatch.

MOUNTAIN CHICKADEE

Mountain Chickadees are small friendly birds, common in conifer forests. They are mostly gray and white with a black cap and bib. Mountain chickadees have white eyebrows, unlike the related Black-capped Chickadee. They nest in cavities in rotting stumps and snags. Chickadees stay for the winter, fluffing up their feathers for extra insulation.

HOUSE WREN

The House Wren is a common, small brown bird with a loud, exuberant song. They compete very aggressively for nest cavities in trees or birdhouses, sometimes throwing out the nest and eggs of another bird in order to use the cavity. Wrens build nests of twigs and grass inside the tree cavities and lay 5 to 8 eggs. In the fall they head south for the winter.

House Wren

51

White-tailed Ptarmigan

WHITE-TAILED PTARMIGAN

The white-tailed ptarmigan is a slow moving, chicken-like grouse of the alpine tundra. It is the only bird that spends the whole year on the tundra. Its summer plumage of mottled brown feathers afford it remarkable camouflage. As winter approaches, the brown feathers are molted and replaced by white ones, so when the snow arrives the ptarmigan is completely white. It has feathers on its feet to keep them warm, and to act as snowshoes. On winter nights, ptarmigan burrow into the snow for insulation.

NORTHERN FLICKER

Northern flickers are common large wood-peckers. There are three varieties of flickers in the nation—the yellow-shafted flicker of the east, the gilded flicker of the southwest, and the red-shafted variety of the west. They reside most anywhere there are trees, sometimes in suburban areas where they torment homeowners by noisily hammering on houses. They are about 12" long, mostly brown with dark bars and spots, and a black bib. The red-shafted flicker has bright salmon-colored wing linings which are visible in flight, and males have red cheek patches. They search for insects on the ground, and are particularly fond of ants. Flickers establish their territories and attract mates by hammering on resonating tree trunks, then drill nest cavities in convenient trees with their strong beaks. The holes they leave are important nesting sites for many other birds.

Red-shafted Flicker at nest with chicks

Male Williamson's Sapsucker   Female Williamson's Sapsucker

54

WILLIAMSON'S SAPSUCKER
RED-NAPED SAPSUCKER

Sapsuckers are medium-sized woodpeckers that live in mountain forests. They can perch tightly on a tree trunk, using their stiff tail feathers as a prop. Sapsuckers use their strong bills to excavate nest cavities in trees. They also drill rows of shallow holes in tree bark, and return to feed on the sap and insects that collect in them.

The male Williamson's sapsucker looks completely different from the female, being mostly black with white facial stripes and wing patches, a yellow belly, and a red throat. The female has a brown head, irregular black striped wings, the yellow belly, and a hint of the red throat. Red-naped sapsuckers are mostly black and white, with red crown and throat patches.

Red-naped Sapsuckers

Killdeer

KILLDEER

The killdeer is a very common shorebird and member of the plover family. It is about ten inches long, with brown wings, white belly, and two black neck stripes. It is found in wetlands as well as far from water in pastures and fields. If a nesting killdeer is threatened, it will try to distract the predator away from its nest. It will act injured, conspicuously dragging itself with apparently broken wings until its nest is safe and it flies away.

AMERICAN AVOCET

Avocets are large, elegant shorebirds that live near marshes and ponds of the lower elevations. They have tan heads, black wings with white stripes, long black upturned bills, and long blue-gray legs. They wade in shallow waters, sweeping their bills side-to-side to dislodge small aquatic animals and insects. In the winter they migrate to the California and Gulf coasts.

American Avocet

White Pelican

WHITE PELICAN

The white pelican is the largest bird in the Rockies. They are mostly white with long orange bills and black tips on their nine-foot wings. With their large wings, they glide easily and can be seen soaring in lazy circles in the sky. Pelicans are fish-eaters, scooping them up with their large bills into their expandable neck pouches. Pelicans nest in colonies on isolated islands. The chicks feed by taking fish from their parents' open bills.

GREAT BLUE HERON

The great blue heron is a large, stately bird, mostly blue-gray with a white head and a long yellow bill. Standing four feet tall, it is the largest and most common heron in the area. Its long legs allow it to wade in shallow water to search for food. A heron hunts by standing motionless until an unsuspecting fish swims by. Then it suddenly plunges its head into the water, snagging a meal. They may also stalk mice and rodents on dry land. In flight, its long neck is folded back into an S-shape, and its feet dangle out behind. Great blue herons nest in groups, reusing the same nests each year.

Great Blue Heron

In the spring, the male Yellow-headed Blackbird perches high in a cattail marsh and sings his raspy song.